THE 5 AM MIRACLE

The 5 AM Miracle

UNLOCKING YOUR MOST PRODUCTIVE SELF

B. Vincent

QuillQuest Publishers

Contents

Introduction

The Force of Mornings

Imagine the world before daybreak: a peaceful place that is practically substantial, roads without any trace of hustle, and the primary light of sunrise penetrating the skyline. This peaceful setting isn't simply a background for writers and visionaries; it's material for the useful and the effective. The force of mornings, particularly those that start at 5 AM, lies in their immaculate potential—when interruptions are snoozing and the day's material is yours to paint.

The early hours offer an interesting mix of quietness and opportunity. In this quietness, your psyche isn't yet attacked by the requests and clamors of the day. It's a second when your inventive resources are more open, not yet hosed by the exhaustion or stress that the day might bring. Studies propose that our minds, straight from a supportive rest, are at their top with regards to innovativeness and insightful reasoning during these early hours. This is when complex issues appear to be less complex, and creative arrangements show up more promptly.

Besides, the demonstration of ascending before the sun is a statement of goal. It's a guarantee to yourself that you will do what most will not—live every moment to the fullest from its actual beginning. This responsibility develops discipline, a characteristic that is crucial to the outcome of any undertaking. Discipline brings forth an endless propensity that shapes the establishment whereupon objectives are envisioned as well as accomplished.

The force of mornings stretches beyond the mental advantages. Physiologically, lining up with the regular world's musicality cultivates a congruity inside. The human body's circadian rhythms, our inward clock, are intended to answer the patterns of constant By awakening with the first light, you're not simply sticking to an efficiency hack; you're embracing a way of life that synchronizes with the actual quintessence of our science, improving mental readiness as well as by and large wellbeing.

Embracing the early morning isn't simply about getting an early advantage on your plan for the day. It's tied in with guaranteeing a space in your day where you can zero in on self-improvement, plan with clarity, and develop a care that will bring you through your other waking hours. It's a period for contemplation, for working out, for perusing—exercises that, in the surge of a commonplace day, may be consigned to the domain of "assuming there's time."

In perceiving the force of mornings, you open a mystery shared by a larger number of the world's best people. They realize that this time isn't a penance, but rather a gift—aa calm hour not taken from rest yet given to reason. As we venture through this book, we'll investigate how to tackle this gift, changing the initial murmurs of first light into an everyday wonder of efficiency, prosperity, and individual accomplishment.

Why 5 AM?

In the ensemble of a typical day's disarray, 5 a.m. stands

apart as a note struck in the calm—aa period that appears to exist outside the surge of hours that follow. In any case, why 5 a.m. explicitly? This hour, frequently proclaimed as the brilliant key to opening a day's maximum capacity, isn't picked with no obvious end goal in mind. Its determination is established in a conversion of science, brain research, and hundreds of years of shrewdness, making it a period yet a groundbreaking practice.

The science behind getting up at 5 a.m. is convincing. Organic examination shows that our cortisol levels, answerable for stress and readiness, normally top soon after arousal. By adjusting our wake-up opportunity to this regular ascent in cortisol, we guarantee that our body's preparation for activity and our brain's ability for sharpness are a unified whole. At 5 AM, the world is still, outside requests are not many, and the spike in cortisol serves not as a response to stretch but rather as a groundwork for useful commitment with the day ahead.

Mentally, getting up at 5 a.m. establishes a vibe of proactivity. A decision positions us in front of the world's requests, not dashing to find them. This proactivity cultivates an outlook of control and deliberateness. At the point when you start your day with reason, that feeling of direction saturates all that you do, transforming customary errands into bits of a bigger objective. The discipline expected to ascend at this hour likewise reinforces determination, which converts into different everyday issues, causing overwhelming assignments to appear to be more sensible.

By and large, a considerable number of the world's most powerful figures have embraced the ethics of an early ascent. From Benjamin Franklin's well-known proverb, "Right on time to bed and right on time to rise, makes a man solid, rich, and insightful," to present-day chiefs and world pioneers beginning their day prior to the sun, the agreement is clear: the early morning hours hold an influence unequaled by some other season of day. These hours are seen as a period for work, yet as a hallowed space for personal growth and reflection that energizes outcomes in any remaining undertakings.

Besides, the decision at 5 a.m. explicitly considers a time of unparalleled serenity. In the predawn hours, interruptions are basically nonexistent. The messages presently can't seem to flood in; the telephone stays quiet. This absence of interference implies your most significant, profound work can happen when your psyche is freshest, without the back-and-forth for your consideration that characterizes later hours.

At last, embracing 5 AM is about something beyond efficiency; it's tied in with prosperity. This hour offers a tranquil span for contemplation, exercise, and setting expectations—rehearse that support both brain and body, establishing the groundwork for a better, more focused life.

Deciding to ascend at 5 AM is, in this manner, a purposeful system to outfit the calm force of the morning, line up with our body's regular rhythms, and set out a plan of deliberateness that directs the remainder of our day. As we dive further into this training, we'll find that the demonstration of waking at 5 AM isn't just about acquiring additional hours; it's tied in with changing each part of our lives by the nature of those hours.

The Study of Efficiency

In our journey to open the most useful self, establishing our practices on the strong bedrock of logical evidence is vital. The early morning hours, especially the period around 5 AM, are not simply emotionally quiet; they are impartially gainful as per an abundance of logical exploration. This part dives into the neuroscience and brain research that support the efficiency marvel of the early morning.

Neuroscience has long concentrated on the rhythms of our mind's action and how these rhythms impact our mental capabilities. One key disclosure is the idea of the mind's maximized execution times, otherwise called chronotypes. While people might have individual varieties, a critical group of examination proposes that for the vast majority, the early morning hours are the point at which the cerebrum is generally open to profound, centered work. During these hours, the prefrontal cortex, liable for independent direction and decisive reasoning, is especially dynamic. This increased movement is the reason assignments that require focus and imagination are, in many cases, best handled not long after we awaken.

Moreover, rest science assumes a basic part in understanding why the 5 AM awakening can be groundbreaking. The nature of our rest cycles directly influences our mental capability and state of mind the next day. By adjusting our wake-up opportunity to the normal finish of our last REM (Quick Eye Development) rest cycle, we can guarantee that we awaken feeling revived and intellectually sharp. Getting up at 5 AM, when finished related to a proper sleep time to guarantee an entire night's rest, can synchronize with these ideal rest cycle endings, improving our mental capacities from the outset of our day.

The mental advantages of early rising are similarly

convincing. Taking part in useful work or self-awareness exercises at 5 a.m. exploits what clinicians call the "new beginning impact." This peculiarity depicts how individuals are bound to participate in objectively situated conduct following transient milestones, like the start of a day, week, or year. The early morning, undisturbed and calm, goes about as an everyday new beginning, a mental reset button that engages us to handle our objectives with restored energy.

Besides, the discipline expected to reliably ascend at 5 AM supports a mental guideline known as self-viability, the confidence in our capacity to prevail in unambiguous circumstances. This conviction is basic for keeping up with inspiration and tirelessness toward long-term objectives. Every morning that you prevail with regards to rising early fortifies your self-viability, making a positive input circle that helps certainty and efficiency across all parts of your life.

Finally, the act of waking up early is upheld by the standard of self-discipline, which is a limited asset that renews with rest. By beginning our day at 5 AM, we tap into our resolve supply at its fullest, empowering us to settle on better choices, oppose enticements, and spotlight our assignments with more noteworthy force. This essential utilization of our determination makes us more useful as well as guarantees that we're applying the best version of ourselves to our most significant work.

In total, the study of efficiency enlightens why the early morning hours are a once-in-a lifetime chance for individual and expert turns of events. Through understanding the neurological, mental, and physiological groundworks of this training, we can all the more likely outfit the force of 5 AM to accomplish unmatched efficiency and satisfaction.

Making way for progress

Leaving on the excursion to turn into a morning person and embracing the 5 AM supernatural occurrence requires something beyond setting a morning timer; it requires an insightful planning of both psyche and climate. This section is committed to the basic advances necessary to change the goal of getting up at 5 AM into a manageable practice. Here, we dig into the mentality shifts, planning procedures, and natural changes that make ready for a consistent progress into early rising, making way for unmatched efficiency and self-awareness.

Outlook Moves: The most important phase in this groundbreaking excursion is a recalibration of our mentality. Embracing the early morning starts with understanding and esteeming its true capacity as a holy time for self-awareness and efficiency. This psychological shift includes seeing the early hours not as a penance but rather as an interest in oneself. Developing a positive relationship with the early morning is pivotal; imagine the tranquil, undisturbed hours as a gift when you can make progress toward your objectives in isolation and harmony. Recognizing the difficulties and changing your point of view to see them as venturing stones as opposed to obstructions is vital to supporting inspiration.

Readiness Methodologies: Progress in getting up at 5 a.m. reliably is not set in stone by the activities required the prior night. A serene night's rest is central, and that implies taking on a trained evening schedule that elevates unwinding and indicates to your body that now is the right time to slow down. This can include restricting screen time, participating in quiet exercises like perusing or contemplation, and guaranteeing an agreeable, rest-friendly climate. Getting ready for the morning ahead—spreading out exercise garments, setting up your workspace, arranging your most memorable assignment—can likewise altogether diminish grating, making the progress from rest to efficiency smoother and really engaging.

Ecological Changes: The climate where we wake assumes a critical role in the way we think about getting up early. Making a space that you anticipate awakening in can extraordinarily upgrade your morning experience. This could include enhancing your room for rest (taking into account factors like light, temperature, and commotion) and planning a morning space that rouses efficiency and quiet. For some's purposes, this implies a devoted work area with insignificant interruptions; for other people, it very well may be a comfortable corner for perusing and reflection.

Saddling Innovation Shrewdly: While innovation can be an interruption, it can likewise act as an incredible asset in supporting your initial rising propensity. Shrewd cautions that reenact dawn or radiate delicate, step-by-step expanding sounds can assist with facilitating the change from rest to alertness. Also, applications that track rest designs or help you remember your nightly schedule can uphold your objective of getting to bed on time and awakening revived.

Building a Strong People Group: Finally, setting out on this excursion close by others, whether through web-based gatherings, responsibility accomplices, or relatives, can give a wellspring of inspiration and backing. Sharing your objectives, difficulties, and victories with a local area of similar people can improve your responsibility and give you significant bits of knowledge and consolation.

Making way for progress at 5 AM is a comprehensive cycle that includes something beyond changing your wake-up time; it requires an exhaustive methodology that incorporates mental, physical, and ecological arrangements. By taking on these procedures, you're preparing yourself to rise right on time as well as to do so with energy and reason, laying the basis for a day loaded up with accomplishment and individual satisfaction.

Embracing the Excursion: Difficulties and Wins

The way to turning into a go-getter, particularly one who welcomes the day at 5 AM with force and design, is full of difficulties. However, it is these very challenges that prepare for critical self-awareness and the many victories that go with an all-around upgraded morning schedule. In embracing this excursion, it's fundamental to recognize the obstacles, gain from them, and praise every triumph, however little it might appear. This last mark of our acquaintance is a confirmation of the flexibility required and the significant feeling of achievement that is standing by.

Expecting and Conquering Snags: The primary long stretches of changing in accordance with a 5 AM awaken can be especially challenging. The body and psyche, familiar with an alternate mood, may oppose this new timetable. You could confront days where the compulsion to hit nap is over-powering or mornings where your efficiency doesn't quickly measure up to your assumptions. Perceiving these minutes as a feature of the cycle is vital. Every hindrance is a potential chance to refine your methodology, whether that implies changing your nighttime schedule for better rest quality or finding additional convincing motivations to start off right on time. Perseverance, matched with an eagerness to adjust, is vital.

The Force of Little Wins: In the beginning phases of your excursion, the significance of celebrating little wins couldn't possibly be more significant. Getting up at 5 AM for sequential days, adhering to your morning schedule, or following through with a responsibility you've decided to do in the early hours are accomplishments that gather speed. These triumphs, regardless of how minor they appear, support your responsibility and lift your certainty. They act as tokens of your capacity and the headway you're making toward turning into your generally useful self.

The Change of Propensity into Custom: Over the long haul, the test of getting up at 5 AM changes from a day-to-day fight into a valued custom. This shift happens as the advantages of your morning schedule become progressively obvious—whether it's through the substantial achievement of objectives, the reliability that goes with the early hours, or the improved feeling of prosperity. The wake-up routine turns into a period you watch enviously, a period committed to personal growth and reflection that you wouldn't swear off.

Exploring Life's Inescapable Changes: Life is dynamic, and there will be periods when keeping a 5 a.m. awake becomes troublesome. Travel, family responsibilities, or unforeseen difficulties might upset your daily practice. These minutes test your strength and adaptability. The key is to move toward such interruptions with effortlessness, adjusting where important while continuously keeping sight of your overall objective. It's not necessary to focus on flawlessness, but on consistency and the capacity to get back to your daily schedule with a recharged center.

Considering the Excursion: As you become more acquainted with your initial morning schedule, reflection turns into a priceless apparatus. Thinking back on where you began, the difficulties you've survived, and the development you've encountered can unquestionably compensate. This reflection serves as inspiration to go on as well as a sign of the groundbreaking force of commitment and discipline.

Embracing the excursion to open your generally useful self at 5 AM is about something other than the demonstration of waking early; it's about the development, difficulties, and wins experienced enroute. Each step, each obstacle, and every triumph is basic to the interaction, forming you into a more focused, centered, and satisfied person. By focusing on this excursion, you are making way for a day-to-day existence where efficiency and individual fulfillment are objectives as well as real factors.

1

Chapter 1: The 5 AM Blueprint

Understanding the Force of 5 AM

The excursion toward opening your most useful self starts in the calm, predawn hours—when the world dozes and potential outcomes stir. The choice to ascend at 5 AM is in excess of a simple change of your morning timer; it's a guarantee to embrace the unmatched quietness and potential that these early hours offer. This section opens with a profound jump into the essence of 5 AM and its groundbreaking power, setting the foundation for the life-changing practices that follow.

At 5 AM, the tranquility of the world isn't simply scenery; it's material. This time is free of any trace of interruptions and requests that will fill the later hours, making it the ideal climate for engaged, continuous work. Whether it's seeking after private tasks, arranging your day, or taking part in taking care of oneself, the early morning offers an extraordinary chance to do so with a clarity and force that is many times impossible once the day completely starts.

Be that as it may, the force of 5 AM reaches out past the shortfall of interruptions. A period empowers reflection and thoughtfulness, permitting you to interface with your deepest considerations and desires without the outer commotion that frequently overwhelms them. In these calm hours, you're not simply working; you're investigating the profundities of your true capacity and making the vision for the existence you seek to lead.

Besides, ascending at 5 AM ingrains a feeling of discipline and reason that can impact each part of your life. The demonstration of getting up while the world is as yet dull is a day-to-day reaffirmation of your obligation to your objectives and your self-improvement. This discipline turns into the foundation of your personality, a characteristic that fortifies your purpose and versatility notwithstanding challenges.

The mental effect of being a go-getter couldn't possibly be more significant. It develops a mentality of proactivity, where you're done responding to the world's requests while effectively molding your day from its actual beginning. This proactive methodology gathers a speed that brings you through the whole day, improving your efficiency and feeling of achievement.

Embracing 5 AM is additionally a demonstration of taking care of oneself. It's a chance to focus on your prosperity and self-improvement before the day's commitments outweigh everything else. Whether through exercise, contemplation, or essentially partaking in the serenity of first light, these early hours become a sacrosanct time for sustaining your physical, mental, and close-to-home wellbeing.

In this section, we dive into the advantages of the 5 a.m. way of life, laying the foundation for a groundbreaking excursion. By understanding the force of this time, you're not simply planning to change your morning; you're making way for a significant change in your life. The excursion to your most useful self starts here, in the tranquil commitment of the early morning.

Making Your Own 5 AM Vision

Leaving on the 5 AM venture isn't about indiscriminately pursuing a direction; it's about deliberately planning a morning that drives you towards your most genuine aspirations and wants. This section digs into the core of making your own 5 AM vision, a significant stage in tackling the extraordinary capability of the early hours. Your vision is the signal that guides you through the quietness of the first light, enlightening your way toward individual and expert satisfaction.

Recognize Your Center Targets: The most important phase in creating your vision is to distinguish what you really need to accomplish in these undisturbed hours. Is it to gain ground on a meaningful venture that has been sidelined by the monotonous routine? Maybe it's to develop a solid body and brain through exercise and contemplation, or, basically, to find a tranquil second for reflection before the day starts. Whatever your objectives, they ought to resound profoundly with your general life yearnings, going about as building blocks for the bigger picture you wish to make.

Picture Your Optimal Morning: With your goals clear,

the subsequent stage is to envision what your ideal 5 a.m. morning resembles. Imagine the exercises that occupy this time, from the second you wake to the arrangements until the end of your day. Perception is an amazing asset for arranging as well as cultivating the inspiration and fervor necessary to make your vision a reality. This envisioned morning shouldn't just line up with your objectives but additionally rouse a feeling of euphoria and expectation.

Adjust Your Vision to Your Qualities: Your 5 a.m. vision ought to be an impression of your own qualities and convictions. Assuming family is fundamental to your life, your initial morning schedule could incorporate calm time for arranging family exercises or composing smart notes to your friends and family. Assuming that self-awareness is your foundation, committing time to acquiring new abilities or perusing moving writing may be key parts of your morning. This arrangement guarantees that your initial hours are useful as well as profoundly satisfying.

Make a Dream Explanation: To set your 5 AM vision, create a compact and rousing vision proclamation. This ought to embody your targets, the embodiment of your optimal morning, and the qualities that guide you. A strong vision proclamation fills in as a day-to-day sign of why you're embracing the 5 AM wonder; giving lucidity and inspiration even on mornings while leaving the solace of your bed feels like an enormous errand.

Embrace adaptability and variation. At last, comprehend that your 5 AM vision isn't firmly established. As you leave on this excursion, you'll more deeply study yourself—what strengthens you, what doesn't function as well as you'd expected, and what new desires arise. Being available to tweak your vision guarantees that your initial mornings keep lining up with your advancing objectives and life conditions.

Making your own 5 AM vision is the foundation of your excursion toward opening your generally useful self. A cycle requests reflection, trustworthiness, and imagination. By characterizing what the early hours mean to you and how they can serve your bigger life objectives, you set up for mornings that are useful as well as profoundly significant.

Beating normal difficulties

Embracing the 5 a.m. way of life is an excursion loaded with difficulties, yet these obstacles are not impossible. They are essentially important for the course of change and development. This part is devoted to recognizing normal obstructions you might experience and giving reasonable techniques to overcome them. By recognizing these difficulties head-on, you can arm yourself with the strength and flexibility expected to make your 5 a.m. marvel an economical piece of your life.

For the overwhelming majority, the greatest deterrent is the demonstration of awakening itself. Progressing to a prior awaken time can be a shock to your framework, particularly in the event that you're familiar with late evenings. To facilitate this change, fire steadily by awakening only 15 minutes sooner every day until you arrive at your 5 a.m. objective. Guarantee your room climate advances peaceful rest, from an agreeable sleeping pad to limiting light and commotion contamination. Likewise, consider a wake-up routine that energizes you, making the demonstration of awakening something to anticipate.

2

Chapter 2: Keeping up with Consistency

Consistency is critical to receiving the rewards of the 5 AM way of life, yet it very well may be hard to support. Life's unpredictability's, like late-night responsibilities or un-expected disturbances, can wreck your daily schedule. To battle this, place emphasis on building major areas of strength for your 5 AM responsibility. Helping yourself to remember the advantages and objectives related to your initial mornings can give you the inspiration you need to keep up with consistency. Moreover, consider adaptability in your timetable as essential, understanding that periodic deviations will not fix your advancement.

Tracking down Inspiration Even with an unmistakable vision, there will be mornings when inspiration is scant. At these times, it's critical to rest on discipline instead of transitory inspiration. Setting up responsibility frameworks, like registrations with a companion or public responsibilities, can reinforce your purpose. Keep in mind that inspiration frequently follows activity. Begin with the littlest step of your morning schedule, and you'll probably track down the energy to proceed.

Managing Lack of Sleep: Early mornings shouldn't come to the detriment of sufficient rest. Assuming you're battling with lack of sleep, reevaluate your evening schedule. Focus on getting sufficient rest by changing your sleep time as per your wake-up time and going for long stretches of rest each evening. This might require forfeiting late-night exercises, yet the advantages of a revived and useful morning offset the impermanent delights of evening relaxation.

Adapting to the Absence of Prompt Outcomes The change into your most useful self is a steady cycle. You may not see quick changes, prompting disappointment and uncertainty. It's vital to celebrate little triumphs and perceive that when you consistently focus on your 5 AM standard, you're establishing an establishment for long-term achievement. Tolerance and steadiness are your partners on this excursion.

In beating these difficulties, recall that the way to opening your most useful self is exceptional for every person. What works for one individual may not work for another, and the key is to find and adjust systems that best suit your way of life and objectives. The 5 AM supernatural occurrence isn't just about getting up ahead of schedule; it's about how you manage that chance to create an existence of direction, efficiency, and individual satisfaction.

The Underpinning of Ceremonies and Schedules

At the center of the 5 AM supernatural occurrence lies the force of ceremonies and schedules. These are not simply errands or things on a plan for the day; they are holy practices that set the vibe for your whole day, instilling it with reason, heading, and energy. This part starts by investigating the basic role that ceremonies and schedules play in changing your initial mornings from a battle to a safe haven of efficiency and self-improvement.

Ceremonies and schedules are the bedrock upon which your 5 AM achievement is constructed. They give structure to the apparently endless time that the early morning offers, directing you through your exercises with expectation and concentration. In any case, their importance reaches beyond simple planning; these practices are permeated with individual significance, changing commonplace assignments into snapshots of care and self-association.

Integrating customs into your morning starts with recognizing exercises that resonate profoundly with you, exercises that add to your efficiency as well as to your prosperity. Whether it's some tea delighted in peacefully, a couple of pages of a rousing book, or a lively stroll to invite the day, these ceremonies ought to be things you anticipate and rehearse that feed your spirit and stir your faculties.

Schedules, then again, are the arrangements of activities that lead you towards accomplishing your objectives. They are the means you take to gain ground on your activities, to really focus on your wellbeing, and to plan for the day ahead. While schedules are more functional in nature than customs, they are no less huge. They are the vehicles that drive you forward, changing your dreams into substantial results.

The production of your wake-up routines and schedules is both a craft and a science. It requires a comprehension of the main thing to you, an enthusiasm for the worth of your time, and a pledge to focus intently on ways that are generally significant. This section will direct you through the most common way of building ceremonies and schedules that upgrade your efficiency as well as improve your life, making every morning a venturing stone for the individual you seek to turn into.

As we dive further into the components of compelling ceremonies and schedules, recall that these practices are profoundly private. What works for one individual may not work for another, and the magnificence of this excursion lies in finding what particularly energizes your spirit and drives your efficiency. The objective isn't to repeat another person's morning, but to make one that is legitimately yours, loaded up with rehearsals that raise your mornings from commonplace to wonderful.

Distinguishing Your Cornerstone Propensities

The subsequent central issue in changing your mornings through ceremonies and schedules centers around the identification and development of cornerstone propensities. Cornerstone propensities are strong on the grounds that they exert a cascading type of influence, setting off a chain response that decidedly influences different parts of your life. By pinpointing and coordinating these propensities into your morning schedule, you upgrade your efficiency as well as encourage enhancements in your general prosperity and life fulfillment.

Understanding Cornerstone Propensities: Cornerstone

propensities are the foundation of successful schedules. They are the propensities that, once settled, have the ability to change your life. These propensities are unique to every person, reflecting individual objectives and values. For some's purposes, a cornerstone propensity may be day-to-day work out, which empowers the body and explains the brain. For other people, it very well may be contemplation or journaling —rehearsals that encourage mental clarity and close-to-home versatility.

The far-reaching influence of cornerstone propensities: The wizardry of cornerstone propensities lies in their gradually expanding influence. At the point when you focus on a cornerstone propensity, it normally prompts the reception of other positive ways of behaving. For instance, people who start their day with exercise may be more disposed to eat soundly or deal with their time more proficiently. The discipline and center acquired from keeping a cornerstone propensity spill over into different regions, making an all-encompassing improvement in your way of life.

Recognizing Your Cornerstone Propensities: To outfit the force of cornerstone propensities, begin by considering the parts of your life you wish to improve or the objectives you mean to accomplish. Consider propensities that would straightforwardly affect these desires. Try different things with various exercises during your morning schedule and see which ones yield the main advantages, both right away and over the long haul.

Coordinating Cornerstone Propensities into Your Daily Practice: Whenever you've distinguished your cornerstone propensities, the subsequent stage is to coordinate them into your morning schedule in a supportable manner. Start by devoting a particular time allotment for these propensities, guaranteeing they get the need they merit. It's vital to begin small, permitting your body and mind to conform to these new practices without feeling overpowered.

The Job of Consistency and Persistence: The development of cornerstone propensities requires consistency and tolerance. These propensities might find an opportunity to lay out, and there will be days when your responsibility is tested. In any case, the way to progress lies in diligence. By reliably focusing on your cornerstone propensities, in any event, when progress appears to be slow, you'll, bit by bit, observe a significant change in your efficiency and individual satisfaction.

Distinguishing and sustaining your cornerstone propensities is an essential move toward making a morning schedule that really resonates with your own and proficient objectives. By zeroing in on these primary propensities, you set up for an outpouring of positive changes, guaranteeing that every morning adds to a more extravagant, seriously satisfying life.

Tweaking Your Morning Schedule

The third support point in the improvement of your extraordinary wake-up routines and schedules focuses on the significance of customization. A morning schedule that catalyzes efficiency and self-awareness isn't one-size-fits-all; it should be customized to accommodate your exceptional way of life, objectives, and inclinations. This segment digs into the workmanship and study of redoing your morning schedule, guaranteeing that it lines up with your singular necessities and desires.

The Meaning of Personalization: The adequacy of your morning schedule is fundamentally improved when it mirrors your own conditions, including your vocation objectives, family obligations, and individual interests. A normal person who is impeccably fit for a solitary businessperson probably won't work for a parent of small kids. In this manner, customization is critical to making a morning schedule that isn't just feasible but additionally pleasant and satisfying.

Evaluation of Individual Objectives and Inclinations: The most important phase in redoing your morning schedule is to direct a careful appraisal of your own objectives and inclinations. What are you wanting to accomplish with your mornings? Might it be said that you are looking to upgrade your efficiency, cultivate self-improvement, or work on your wellbeing and health? Understanding your essential targets will guide you in choosing exercises that are generally aligned with your objectives.

Thought of Natural and Chrono typical Elements: Every individual has an extraordinary organic clock, or chronotype, that impacts their ideal times for resting, waking, and working. Certain individuals are normally ambitious, while others track down their pinnacle efficiency later in the day. Tweaking your morning schedule includes considering these variables and planning a timetable that follows your normal rhythms, subsequently expanding your energy and productivity.

Joining of Adaptability: A vital part of a tweaked morning schedule is adaptability. Life is capricious, and your routine ought to be sufficiently versatile to accommodate unanticipated changes or crises. Consolidating cushion times, elective exercises, and "plan B" choices guarantees that your morning schedule stays powerful, in any event, when the unforeseen happens.

Iterative Refinement: At long last, the customization of your morning schedule is a continuous cycle. As your life conditions change, so too should your daily schedule. Consistently audit and refine your morning exercises to guarantee they keep on serving your developing objectives and inclinations. Explore different avenues regarding new propensities, dispose of what no longer serves you, and constantly enhance your everyday practice for the greatest effect.

Tweaking your morning schedule is a dynamic and individual excursion. By adjusting your morning exercises to your singular necessities and objectives, you create a strong starting point for progress. This custom-fitted methodology improves your efficiency as well as enhances your life, making every morning a venturing stone toward achieving your fullest potential.

The Job of Climate in Forming Your Morning Schedule

The fourth basic part of creating a successful morning schedule revolves around the climate in which it unfolds. The spaces where we reside and work significantly affect our mindsets, energy levels, and efficiency. This part investigates how to purposefully plan your current circumstances to help and upgrade your wake-up routines and schedules, transforming your environmental elements into a partner as you continue looking for an extraordinary beginning to your day.

Making a Favorable Morning Space: The climate where you start your day can essentially impact how you feel and perform. A jumbled, turbulent space can prompt sensations of stress and overwhelm, while a perfect, coordinated climate can cultivate clarity and inspiration. Begin by making a morning space that is committed to your ceremonies and schedules, whether it's a calm corner for contemplation, a sufficiently bright work area for arranging your day, or a kitchen arrangement that welcomes smart dieting. This space ought to indicate to your cerebrum that now is the right time to take part in your morning rehearsals.

The Significance of Negligible Interruptions: In the present-associated world, interruptions are ever-present. To take full advantage of your morning schedule, limiting these distractions is vital. This could mean keeping your telephone in off-line mode, utilizing applications that block virtual entertainment, or defining limits with relatives during your holy morning time. By diminishing interferences, you permit yourself to draw in with your ceremonies and schedules, extending their effect and viability completely.

Utilizing Normal Light and Outside Air: The advantages of regular light and natural air for our prosperity are factual. Integrating these components into your morning schedule can significantly improve your sharpness and mindset. If conceivable, position your morning space close to a window, or, assuming it doesn't rain, remove a portion of your standard outside. The openness to regular light controls your circadian rhythms, while outside air strengthens the faculties, giving a characteristic increase in energy and motivation.

Customizing Your Space: Individual contacts can change your morning space from just useful to profoundly moving. Consider adding components that spark euphoria and inspiration, for example, persuasive statements, individual tokens, or a dream board. These individual contacts make your morning space really yours, establishing a climate that elevates and propels you to handle the day ahead with energy and concentration.

The Effect of Routine on Natural Plans: On the other hand, your morning schedule can impact how you plan and communicate with your current circumstances. As you refine your customs and schedules, you could wind up making changes to your space to all the more likely oblige these practices. This unique exchange between routine and climate is a demonstration of the developing idea of self-improvement and efficiency. By ceaselessly adjusting your environmental elements to help your morning rehearsals, you create a pattern of uplifting feedback that drives you toward your objectives.

Making a climate that upholds your morning schedule isn't just about actual space; it's tied in with making a safe haven for self-improvement and efficiency. By purposefully planning your environmental elements to line up with your customs and schedules, you set up for a morning that not only moves you into your day with energy and concentration but additionally supports your prosperity and motivates your best work.

Embracing Care and Presence

The last foundation for laying out extraordinary ceremonies and schedules lies in the act of care and presence. This isn't just about what you do in the mornings; it's also about the way that you make it happen. Connecting completely with every snapshot of your routine can fundamentally upgrade its advantages, transforming even the least complex assignments into significant encounters of self-improvement and mindfulness.

The Pith of Care In the first part of the day: Care includes giving full consideration to the current second, without judgment. With regards to your morning standard, this implies being completely drawn in by every action, whether it's tasting your espresso, extending your body, or arranging your day. This training assists with mooring you in the now, diminishing pressure, and expanding your appreciation for the little delights of life.

The Force of Ceremonies: Changing pieces of your every-day practice into customs can instill them with more profound significance and fulfillment. A custom is any movement performed with aim and mindfulness. By hoisting routine undertakings to the situation with customs, you carry a feeling of holiness to your mornings. This could be pretty much as basic as lighting a candle while you journal or pausing for a minute to offer thanks prior to beginning your day. These customs help to develop a feeling of direction and appreciation, enhancing your life beyond the limits of efficiency.

Developing Presence through Breath: One of the easiest yet most remarkable ways of developing care and presence is through your breath. Taking profound, cognizant breaths can focus your psyche, decrease uneasiness, and increase your energy levels. Integrating breathing activities into your morning schedule can act as an establishment for a day lived with more noteworthy tranquility and concentration.

The Advantages of Dialing Back: In a culture fixated on speed and proficiency, embracing gradualness in your morning schedule can be progressive. Permitting yourself to play out each undertaking at a relaxed speed without hurrying to the next thing on your plan can fundamentally upgrade your feeling of prosperity and control. This approach not only works on the nature of your morning exercises, but also sets a more conscious and careful tone until the end of your day.

Combination into day-to-day existence: a definitive objective of rehearsing care and presence in your morning schedule is to broaden these characteristics into the remainder of your day. The morning fills in as a preparation ground for living every second with more prominent mindfulness and appreciation. As you become more proficient at connecting completely with your morning exercises, you'll find it simpler to apply a similar degree of presence to errands, cooperations, and difficulties over the course of your day.

Embracing care and presence changes your morning schedule from a progression of errands to be finished into a significant excursion of self-disclosure and development. By putting your complete focus and goal into every second, you not only upgrade the advantages of your wake-up routines and schedules but additionally develop a more extravagant, seriously satisfying life.

3

Chapter 3: Health and Wellness

The Underpinnings of Actual Wellbeing

At the core of each and every useful day, at the center of individual accomplishment and satisfaction, lies the bedrock of actual wellbeing. It's a reality too major to even consider neglecting: the condition of our bodies significantly impacts the limits of our brains. This section opens with an investigation into why actual prosperity isn't simply a piece of a balanced life, but the foundation upon which we fabricate our most useful selves.

Actual well-being is the focal point through which we experience the world. A body that is very well liked, supported, and rested offers a vantage point that is clear, engaged, and prepared to handle the difficulties and potential open doors that every day presents. Alternately, dismissing our actual prosperity can cloud our discernment, lessen our energy, and block our capacity to perform at our pinnacle. The association between a sound body and an upgraded mind isn't only correlational; it is causal. The consideration we put into our actual selves directly impacts our psychological clarity, close-to-home strength, and generally efficiency.

This part dives into the three mainstays of actual wellbeing: exercise, nourishment, and rest. Every support point supports and upgrades the others, creating an all-encompassing structure for health. Workout, past its advantages to heart wellbeing and muscle strength, is a strong energizer for the mind. It improves mental capability, raises state of mind, and hones center, making it a fundamental part of any morning schedule pointed toward amplifying efficiency.

Sustenance, in the interim, fills in as the fuel that drives this finely tuned machine. The food sources we decide to eat can either impel us forward with imperativeness and force or burden us with exhaustion and haze. A fair eating regimen, rich in supplements, gives us the energy expected to support us through demanding days, guaranteeing that our psyches stay sharp and cautious.

Rest, the third support point, is the establishment's bedrock. Quality rest revives the body, fixes muscle and tissue, and resets the cerebrum, setting us up for the difficulties of another day. It is during these serene hours that our bodies unite recollections, process feelings, and revive. The effect of rest on wellbeing and efficiency couldn't possibly be more significant; it is as basic to our prosperity as the air we relax in.

Understanding the exchange between these three support

points is the most important phase in opening ourselves to our most useful selves. By focusing on our actual wellbeing, we set up for a daily existence lived longer, yet entirely more full and extravagant. A daily existence where every day is welcomed not with fear but rather with expectation, prepared to immediately jump all over the chances it offers. This section lays the foundation for a comprehensive way to deal with health, underscoring that to genuinely succeed in our undertakings, we should initially focus on the vessel that brings us through them: our bodies.

Practice as an Impetus for Energy and Mental Clearness

Chasing our most useful selves, practice arises as an active work, however, as a significant impetus for mental and close-to-home restoration. This segment digs into the extraordinary force of development, revealing insight into how standard active work fills in as a foundation for improving our actual capacities as well as lifting our psychological clarity and energy levels.

The enchantment of activity lies in its capacity to conjure an outpouring of biochemical responses inside our bodies. Endorphins, frequently alluded to as the body's normal pain relievers, are delivered during actual work, prompting a raised state of mind and a more uplifting perspective on life. This biochemical shift is supplemented by an expansion in cerebrum-determined neurotrophic factor (BDNF), a protein that upholds the development and separation of new neurons and neurotransmitters. The outcome is a more honed, more engaged mind, prepared to handle complex undertakings with expanded effectiveness and inventiveness.

Coordinating activity into your morning schedule establishes a powerful vibe for the day ahead. A morning run, yoga meeting, or even an energetic walk can light your digestion, launching your body into a condition of elevated sharpness and status. This flood in energy isn't transitory; however, it is maintained, helping you during that time with a consistent stockpile of imperativeness that upgrades your capacity to focus and stay useful during overstretched periods.

Besides, practice is certainly not a one-size-fits-all remedy. Its advantages are open through a wide exhibit of exercises custom-made to fit individual inclinations and ways of life. Whether it's the quiet accuracy of Kendo, the invigorating surge of intense cardio exercise (HIIT), or the trained stances of Pilates, each type of activity offers one-of-a kind advantages that add to mental lucidity and actual prosperity.

The excellence of integrating exercise into your normal untruths lies in the actual change as well as in the psychological flexibility it constructs. Ordinary active work shows discipline, persistence, and responsibility—characteristics that are adaptable to each part of life. It supports the idea that through reliable exertion, we can overcome impediments, accomplish our objectives, and reach our maximum capacity.

As we investigate the diverse advantages of activity, obviously its job reaches out a long way past actual wellness. It is an imperative part of a comprehensive way to deal with well-being, offering a pathway to a more empowered, centered, and useful self. By embracing active work as a day-to-day custom, we don't simply change our bodies; we lift our psyches, making way for a day loaded with achievement and satisfaction.

Nourishment: Energizing Your Body for Max Operation

In the excursion toward opening our most useful selves, nourishment holds a significant job, going about as the fuel that powers both our physical and mental motors. This segment digs into the unpredictable connection between the food varieties we devour and our general presentation, showing how a careful way to deal with eating can essentially upgrade our energy levels, mental clarity, and capacity to center.

At the center of this conversation is the idea that not all food sources are equivalent. Similarly, just as a superior execution vehicle requires premium fuel to work at its ideal, our bodies need the right blend of supplements to ideally work. The right food varieties can raise our smartness, help our energy, and settle our states of mind, consequently empowering us to handle the difficulties of our day with life and accuracy.

An eating routine rich in entire, supplement-rich food sources goes about as the establishment for maximized operation. Food sources that are high in cancer prevention agents, nutrients, and minerals support the mind, improving mental capabilities and safeguarding against oxidative pressure. Complex sugars, lean proteins, and solid fats provide support for energy, forestalling the early afternoon crashes that can wreck our efficiency. Besides, hydration assumes a basic role in this situation. Water, the most ignored supplement, is fundamental for keeping up with fixation and mental capability. Indeed, even gentle parchedness can disable execution, making normal liquid admission over the course of the day a non-debatable component of an efficiency-enhancing diet.

This part likewise addresses the timing and pieces of feasts, offering procedures for dinner arrangements that line up with our body's regular rhythms. It investigates how breakfast can kick off our digestion and set the vibe for the afternoon, why uniformly dispersed feasts can keep up with energy levels, and how key eating can keep our psyches sharp between dinners. Also, it addresses the significance of paying attention to our body's appetite prompts and abstaining from indulging, which can prompt dormancy and diminished center.

Embracing a comprehensive way to deal with sustenance isn't about severe eating, fewer carbs, or hardship; it's about pursuing informed decisions that help our psychological and actual prosperity. Perceiving food as an incredible asset can improve our exhibition, state of mind, and general wellbeing. By choosing food varieties that fuel our bodies effectively, we work on our actual wellbeing as well as make way for a more useful and satisfying day.

As we finish up this investigation of sustenance's part in our efficiency, obviously, the way to our most useful selves is as much about what we eat as all things considered about how we work and rest. Embracing sustenance as the foundation of our day-to-day schedule engages us to accomplish our objectives with energy, clarity, and concentration, preparing for progress in each undertaking.

Rest: The Uncelebrated Yet Truly Great Individual of Efficiency

In the mission to open our most useful selves, rest arises not as an extravagance but rather as an essential mainstay of wellbeing and prosperity. Frequently ignored in a culture that celebrates hecticness, this segment repositions itself at the very front of our efficiency procedure, highlighting its significant effect on our smartness, close-to-home strength, and, generally speaking, execution.

Rest, a long way from being a detached condition of inertia, is a powerful cycle during which our bodies go through a fix, our minds solidify recollections, and our close-to-home encounters are handled. It's the point at which the cerebrum gets out of the messiness of the day, accounting for new data and experiences. The quality and amount of our rest directly impact our mental capabilities, including our capacity to focus, decide, and take care of issues. A very refreshed mind is more honed, more innovative, and more fit for exploring the intricacies of day-to-day existence.

This part dives into the study of rest, making sense of how various phases of rest add to our general prosperity. It features the significance of REM (fast eye development) rest in profound guideline and memory solidification, and how profound rest assumes an essential part in actual recuperation and detoxification of the cerebrum. By understanding the repeating idea of rest stages, we can see the value of why disturbing these cycles can prompt diminished efficiency and decreased wellbeing.

The conversation reaches out to pragmatic exhortations on developing solid rest propensities, or rest cleanliness. It investigates systems for upgrading our rest climate, for example, keeping a cool, dull, and calm room and laying out an unwinding pre-rest routine to indicate to our bodies that now is the right time to slow down. The section additionally addresses normal disruptors of rest, including the effect of electronic gadgets and blue light on our rest wake cycle, and offers answers for moderating these impacts.

Besides, this part underscores the significance of consistency in our rest plans. Hitting the hay and awakening simultaneously every day supports our normal circadian rhythms, upgrading the nature of our rest and, likewise, our day-to-day efficiency. It disperses the legend that we would be able to "get up to speed" with fretted, featuring rather the aggregate idea of lack of sleep and its drawn-out results on our well-being and execution.

By lifting rest to its legitimate spot in our efficiency armory, we not only upgrade our capacity to work at our best during waking hours but additionally support our drawn-out wellbeing and prosperity. Embracing rest as the overlooked yet truly great individual of efficiency permits us to move toward every day with recharged energy, concentration, and flexibility, prepared to handle our objectives with certainty and power.

Care and stress The Board: The Equilibrium Inside

In the scene of efficiency, mental health assumes a basic part, frequently going about as the key part that keeps intact our ability for supported elite execution. This part investigates the significant effect of care and stress on our wellbeing, prosperity, and efficiency. It exposes how developing a careful way to deal with our day-to-day routines can upgrade concentration, strength, and close-to-home balance, in this way opening up our most useful selves.

Care, the act of being completely present and taking part in the occasion without judgment, is in excess of a contemplation procedure—it is a lifestyle. This part examines how incorporating care into our day-to-day schedules can hone our concentration, work on mental adaptability, and diminish the psychological mess that frequently hampers efficiency. By cultivating attention to our viewpoints and sentiments, we figure out how to explore our inner scenes with elegance, perceiving stressors and interruptions without being overpowered by them.

The story then, at that point, moves to the unmistakable advantages of pressure on the board, underscoring that pressure, while an inescapable piece of life, doesn't need to wreck our efficiency. Through down-to-earth systems like profound breathing activities, moderate muscle unwinding, and perception methods, we can figure out how to alleviate the physiological and mental impacts of pressure. These devices not only assist in keeping up with quiet and concentration despite challenges, but additionally save our energy for the errands that make the biggest difference.

Besides, this segment digs into the significance of close-to-home versatility—the capacity to return from difficulties and keep an inspirational perspective. Building flexibility includes encouraging a development outlook, developing appreciation, and rehearsing self-sympathy. It's tied in with perceiving our inborn strength and ability to adjust, which thusly fills our efficiency and drives us towards our objectives.

The section additionally investigates the idea of a balance between fun and serious activities, highlighting the need to make limits between expert and individual lives. It features how care and stress management strategies can assist with keeping up with these limits, guaranteeing that we remain empowered, drawn in, and powerful in all parts of life. By achieving amicable equilibrium, we protect our psychological and actual wellbeing, establishing a strong starting point for feasible efficiency.

In finishing up this investigation of care and stress on the board, obviously the excursion to our most useful selves isn't exclusively about improving our outside climate yet additionally about sustaining our interior world. By embracing care, overseeing pressure really, and keeping up with profound equilibrium, we open a condition of stream where efficiency thrives. This comprehensive methodology not only improves our capacity to accomplish our objectives but additionally enhances our general personal satisfaction, validating that efficiency encompasses both doing and being.

4

Chapter 4 The 5 AM Miracle: Unlocking Your Most Productive Self

Time Usage Dominance

Dominating time effectively is much the same as acquiring a superpower in the mission for efficiency. Perceiving time, in contrast to most assets, is non-sustainable. Once it's spent, it can't be recovered. This acknowledgment shapes the bedrock of our way to deal with augmenting efficiency, directing us to pursue more cognizant decisions about how we dispense our most valuable resource.

The Craft of Prioritization

The excursion starts with the specialty of prioritization.

Not all assignments are made equivalent; some have the ability to move us towards our objectives, while others just keep us occupied. The key is to recognize these two, zeroing in our energy on exercises that offer the best profit from venture. Methods like the Eisenhower Grid assist us with ordering assignments in view of criticality and significance, empowering us to handle the main thing first.

Dispensing with Time-Squanderers

Distinguishing and wiping out time-squanderers is the next basic step. These are the exercises that gobble up our time yet contribute practically nothing to our general targets. Whether it's careless looking at online entertainment, going to pointless gatherings, or capitulating to the bait of performing various tasks, perceiving these entanglements permits us to recover important hours and commit them to intentional activity.

Saddling Time-Usage Devices

In this period of mechanical headway, plenty of devices and strategies stand prepared to help our time usage tries. From computerized schedules that hold our timetables within proper limits to the Pomodoro Method, which breaks work into centered stretches, these apparatuses are intended to upgrade our efficiency. By utilizing these assets, we can find an organized way to deal with our day, guaranteeing that every hour is used to its fullest potential.

The Significance of Reflection

Be that as it may, dominating using time effectively isn't exclusively about the outside demonstration of putting together undertakings; it's likewise about inside reflection. Consistently evaluating how we invest our energy offers important bits of knowledge for our efficiency designs. It prompts us to find out if our everyday exercises line up with our drawn-out objectives and, if not, what shifts are important to address direction.

Living Purposefully

Eventually, time usage dominance is tied to living purposefully. It's a promise to pursue conscious decisions with our time, guaranteeing that each activity we undertake is a stride towards our imagined future. By dominating this discipline, we open our most useful selves as well as make a day-to-day existence that is wealthy in accomplishment and satisfaction.

This section lays the groundwork for an extraordinary way to deal with efficiency, one that regards time as the limited asset it is. Outfitted with the standards of time usage authority, we are better prepared to explore the intricacies of our day-to-day routines, making the most of each and every second towards the acknowledgment of our fantasies.

Objective Setting and Accomplishment

In the orchestra of efficiency, objective setting, and accomplishment are the songs that guide our activities, pervading them with reason and course. This section digs into the nuanced craft of defining significant objectives and the essential excursion toward acknowledging them. It's a pathway set apart by clarity, responsibility, and persistent development.

Characterizing Your Vision

The underlying move toward this interaction is characterizing your vision. What do you try to accomplish? Objectives ought to be something other than passing wishes; they should be clear, explicit, and lined up with your most profound qualities. This clarity serves as a reference point, directing your endeavors and assisting you with exploring through interruptions and impediments. Whether it's progressing in your profession, working on your wellbeing, or dominating another expertise, every objective ought to reflect a veritable longing to develop and get to the next level.

Shrewd Objectives: A System for Progress

To change vision into noteworthy targets, we go to the Savvy rules: explicit, quantifiable, reachable, important, and time-bound. This system guarantees that objectives are distinct and identifiable, giving a reasonable guide to progress. An objective explained as "increment my understanding propensity" becomes "read 24 books in a year, averaging two books each month." This particularity makes the objective more unmistakable as well as works on the most common way of following headway and adapting.

Separating Obstructions

Accomplishing grandiose objectives frequently requires separating them into more modest, reasonable undertakings. This approach assists with demystifying the way to accomplishment, making it not so overwhelming but rather more receptive. By laying out small objectives or achievements, you make a progression of feasible advances that gradually work towards your bigger goal. This division additionally gives normal open doors to reflection and festivity, key parts of keeping up with inspiration.

The Pattern of Survey and Transformation

Objective setting is certainly not a one-time occasion, but rather a unique cycle. Customary surveys permit you to evaluate progress, celebrate victories, and recalibrate techniques on a case-by-case basis. Life's flightiness might require changes in accordance with your arrangements, yet rather than survey these as difficulties, they ought to be embraced as any open doors to refine your methodology. This pattern of arrangement, activity, assessment, and transformation is the heartbeat of powerful objective accomplishment.

Developing Constancy and Versatility

In conclusion, the excursion toward objective accomplishment is frequently fraught with difficulties. Tirelessness and versatility become important partners, powering your drive to push forward in any event when confronted with difficulties. It's tied in with embracing the mentality that each deterrent is a stepping stone to more noteworthy development and learning. Praising every achievement, regardless of how little, builds up your responsibility and supports your purpose to arrive at the end goal.

In blending these components, objective setting and accomplishment arise as more than simple efficiency strategies; they are groundbreaking cycles that shape our excursion towards greatness. By embracing an organized, deliberate way to deal with our desires, we improve our ability to accomplish as well as extend our excursion into individual and expert turns of events.

Utilizing innovation for productivity

In the computerized age, innovation remains a double-edged sword in the domain of efficiency. On one hand, it offers remarkable chances to smooth out undertakings, upgrade correspondence, and oversee time all the more successfully. On the other hand, it presents a maze of interruptions fit for wrecking centers and weakening endeavors. This part explores the complex equilibrium of outfitting innovation as a strong partner in our mission to boost efficiency while defending against its likely traps.

The Force of Efficiency Applications

The advanced commercial center is loaded with devices intended to improve each feature of our own and proficient lives. From task supervisors like Todoist and Asana that keep our undertakings and cutoff times in clear view to schedule applications that guarantee our timetables are meticulously coordinated, innovation can altogether improve our productivity. These devices offer more than simple comfort; they provide an organized structure inside which our efficiency can prosper.

Altering your tech tool stash

The way to successfully utilize innovation lies in customization. The most useful tech stack is one that lines up with your particular requirements and work processes. It includes a course of determination and refinement, picking applications and programming that seamlessly integrate into your day-to-day schedules. Whether it's a note-taking application that synchronizes across all gadgets or a center clock that wards off the enticement of delaying, the right mix of instruments can change your efficiency.

Exploring the Computerized Interruption Minefield

While innovation offers a way to upgrade efficiency, it likewise represents a huge gamble of interruption. Web-based entertainment, texting, and the perpetual scope of the web can undoubtedly redirect consideration from significant work. Perceiving this is essential to carrying out procedures that limit computerized interference. This could include utilizing site blockers during work hours, setting explicit times for browsing messages, or taking on an innovation-free morning schedule to develop concentration and lucidity.

Embracing Mechanization

One of the most powerful benefits of innovation is its capacity to robotize redundant assignments. From booking messages to computerizing bill installments, setting up frameworks that handle routine undertakings can let loose critical measures of time and mental energy. This section investigates how to distinguish open doors for robotization in both individual and expert settings, empowering you to devote more assets to high-esteem exercises.

The Human Component in a Computerized World

At last, it's memorable fundamental that innovation, for every one of its advantages, is an instrument to improve human efficiency, not supplant it. A definitive objective is to involve innovation that enhances your assets, makes up for your shortcomings, and permits you additional significant investment for inventive and significant work. Keeping a human-driven approach guarantees that innovation serves us, not the other way around.

By decisively coordinating innovation into our efficiency tool compartment, we can open new degrees of productivity and adequacy. This section gives a guide to settling on informed decisions about the computerized instruments we utilize, guaranteeing that innovation goes about as a scaffold for our objectives as opposed to an obstruction.

The Specialty of Appointment and Cooperation

Chasing boosting efficiency, the specialty of designation and cooperation arises as a foundation standard, changing the manner in which we approach undertakings and tasks. This part unfurls the nuanced methodologies for successfully conveying liabilities and saddling the aggregate qualities of a group. It's an excursion from the performance try of overseeing undertakings to the orchestra of collaboration, where the total is more prominent than its parts.

Grasping the Force of Appointment

Assignment isn't simply about offloading errands; it's tied in with perceiving that specific undertakings can be better performed by others, liberating you to zero in on regions where you have the best effect. It starts with the affirmation of one's cutoff points and the comprehension that joint effort can prompt prevalent results. This part investigates the mental boundaries to designation, like the longing for control or apprehension about reduced quality, and offers methodologies to defeat these difficulties.

Distinguishing Delegable Errands

The way to a compelling appointment lies in recognizing which assignments to designate. This includes an insightful investigation of your errands, recognizing those that require your exceptional abilities and those that can be effectively achieved by others. We dig into the models for choosing delegable assignments, underscoring the significance of clarity in results, cycles, and assumptions to guarantee fruitful appointments.

The Craft of Picking the Ideal Public

Appointing successfully requires coordinating undertakings with the ideal individuals, taking into account their abilities, interests, and formative necessities. This section talks about how to survey the qualities and shortcomings of colleagues and adjust undertakings to their capacities and development directions. It highlights the significance of confidence in appointments, outlining how enabling others can prompt expanded inspiration and commitment.

Correspondence and Backing in Designation

Compelling appointments are supported by clear correspondence and continuous help. This includes articulating what should be finished as well as why it is important, giving the specific circumstances and meaning of the errand. We cover the basics of setting clear assumptions, giving important assets, and laying out criticism circles to screen progress and address difficulties as they emerge.

Encouraging a culture of coordinated effort

At last, boosting efficiency through designation and joint effort requires developing a culture where collaboration and common help are valued. This part features the advantages of cultivating a cooperative climate, from upgrading inventiveness and development to dispersing responsibility all the more equally. It offers commonsense ways to construct a group dynamic that energizes open correspondence, shared regard, and shared liability.

In summary, this section raises the ideas of designation and coordinated effort from simple efficiency procedures to the basic components of an effective, hard-working attitude. It gives a diagram for utilizing the aggregate qualities of a group, guaranteeing that errands are finished, however cultivated in a way that enhances both the individual and the system. Through appointment and joint effort, we open the maximum capacity of our aggregate limit, making us ready for unrivaled efficiency and development.

5

Chapter 5: Mindset and Motivation

Developing a Developmental Mentality

At the core of supported efficiency and self-improvement lies a crucial mental idea: the development outlook. This part sets out on an excursion to investigate how developing a development mentality—the conviction that capacities and knowledge can be created through devotion and difficult work—fills in as the bedrock for opening our most useful selves.

The Force of Conviction

The excursion starts with figuring out the extraordinary force of conviction. Our convictions about our own capacities essentially impact how we approach difficulties, misfortunes, and learning opportunities. A development mentality blossoms with the reason that each experience is a venturing stone to progress, cultivating strength and an eagerness to embrace the unexplored world. This segment digs into the science behind outlook and its effect on execution, showing how a change in context can prompt significant changes in our way to deal with work and life.

Beating the Decent Attitude Traps

A considerable number of us, sooner or later, end up entrapped by the proper outlook—the conviction that our capacities are static and unchangeable. This outlook breeds dread of disappointment, evasion of difficulties, and a hesitance to invest energy, considering it to be vain despite inborn constraints. This part recognizes normal fixed outlook traps and offers procedures for defeating them, making ready for a more versatile and strong way to deal with individual and expert development.

Embracing Difficulties

A sign of the development mentality is the hug of difficulties as any open doors for development. Rather than avoiding troublesome undertakings or new pursuits because of a paranoid fear of disappointment, people with a development outlook make a plunge with the comprehension that work prompts dominance. This part gives viable counsel for reorienting our way to deal with difficulties, empowering perusers to search out and draw in with valuable open doors that stretch their capacities and encourage advancement.

The Job of Perseverance

Constancy is the backbone of the development attitude. The quality permits us to continue to push forward, in any event, when progress appears to be slow or impediments seem impossible. This piece of the section investigates the significance of coarseness and assurance, displaying how perseverance, even with mishaps, can prompt leaps forward and accomplishments that appeared to be far off.

Developing a Culture of Development

At last, encouraging a development outlook isn't simply a singular undertaking; developing a climate supports development and learning among companions, family, and partners. This segment offers bits of knowledge about making a culture of development where input is esteemed, triumphs are praised, and disappointments are seen as opportunities for growth. By advancing a development mentality inside our networks, we upgrade our own efficiency as well as add to a stronger, more versatile, and more creative group.

In synopsis, developing a development outlook is about something beyond efficiency; it's tied in with setting the establishment for an existence of constant learning, flexibility, and satisfaction. This section furnishes perusers with the information and devices to embrace difficulties, defeat misfortunes, and, at last, understand their fullest potential.

Tackling the Force of Positive Reasoning

Setting out on the journey for supported inspiration and a useful mentality, the force of positive reasoning arises as a fundamental power. This part dives into the groundbreaking capability of sustaining a hopeful viewpoint, not as a simple, great procedure but rather as a crucial way to deal with confronting life's difficulties and accomplishing objectives.

The Study of Positive Thinking

The investigation starts with a plunge into the science behind confidence, uncovering what an inspirational perspective can mean for everything from our mental flexibility to our actual wellbeing. Studies have shown that hopeful people are more joyful and will generally find actual success in their own and proficient undertakings. This segment looks at the neurological and mental systems through which positive reasoning shapes our world, impacting our ability to tackle issues, explore mishaps, and take advantage of chances.

Reexamining Difficulties

At the center of positive reasoning is the capacity to reexamine difficulties and mishaps as open doors for development and learning. This part frames pragmatic strategies for mental rebuilding, a technique used to move negative idea designs towards additional positive, valuable viewpoints. By changing how we decipher occasions, we can altogether adjust our closeness to home and conduct reactions, changing hindrances into venturing stones toward progress.

The job of appreciation

Appreciation plays a critical role in developing a positive outlook. This part investigates the act of appreciation and its significant consequences for our psychological and close-to-home prosperity. By zeroing in on what we are grateful for, we shift our consideration away from shortage and cynicism towards overflow and appreciation. Pragmatic ways to coordinate appreciation into day-to-day existence, like keeping an appreciation diary or communicating thanks to other people, are given to assist perusers with fostering a more grateful and hopeful viewpoint.

Imagining Achievement

Representation is an integral asset for encouraging positive reasoning and inspiration. This section guides perusers through the most common way of picturing their objectives and the means expected to accomplish them. By making a striking mental picture of progress, people can expand their concentration, inspiration, and certainty. This part offers systems for powerful perception, underscoring the significance of integrating feeling and tactile subtleties to improve the authenticity and effect of psychological symbolism.

Developing Flexibility

The last piece of the puzzle in tackling the force of positive reasoning is developing versatility—the capacity to quickly return from difficulty. This part examines how an inspirational perspective can support versatility, empowering people to explore the high points and low points of existence with elegance and assurance. Techniques for building flexibility, including fostering serious areas of strength for an organization, rehearsing self-sympathy, and keeping a drawn-out point of view, are illustrated to furnish perusers with the abilities expected to flourish despite difficulties.

In synopsis, this part enlightens us on the significant effect of positive reasoning on our outlook and inspiration. By embracing hopefulness, rethinking difficulties, rehearsing appreciation, picturing achievement, and developing flexibility, perusers are engaged to move toward their own and proficient lives with a reestablished feeling of direction and plausibility.

Putting forth and achieving significant objectives

The way to opening our most useful selves is clear with the objectives we set and the responsibility we show towards accomplishing them. This section of the part dives profoundly into the craftsmanship and study of laying out significant objectives and the techniques expected to see them to completion. It's not just about laying out targets; it's about creating a dream for our lives that resonates with our most profound qualities and yearnings.

The Significance of Lucidity

The excursion starts with clarity. This segment underscores the meaning of characterizing clear, succinct objectives. Clearness goes about as the signal of light directing our way through the obscurity of day-to-day interruptions and difficulties. It includes something other than understanding what we need; it requests a profound comprehension of why we need it. This piece of the section guides perusers through practices intended to uncover their actual cravings and the hidden inspirations driving them, guaranteeing that the objectives set are clear as well as profoundly associated with their own qualities and yearnings.

Brilliant Objectives: A Structure for Progress

When the underpinning of clarity is laid out, the center moves to the Savvy system—an abbreviation for explicit, quantifiable, reachable, significant, and time-bound. This part separates every part of the shrewd models, representing how it contributes to making objectives that are distinct as well as reasonable and achievable. Through models and commonsense activities, perusers are told the best way to apply the Savvy system to their own objectives, changing obscure goals into significant plans.

The Force of Steady Advancement

Accomplishing significant objectives is, in many cases, a long-distance race, not a run. This section supports the force of gradual advancement, featuring the significance of separating all-encompassing objectives into more modest, sensible errands. It presents the idea of "miniature objectives," small advances that altogether lead to critical accomplishments. By zeroing in on each little activity in turn, we can keep up with force and stay away from the overpower that frequently goes with the quest for enormous aspirations. This segment gives methodologies for distinguishing and carrying out miniature objectives, guaranteeing consistent advancement towards the bigger vision.

Defeating Impediments

No way to progress is without obstacles. This section tends to the inescapable difficulties and misfortunes one experiences on the excursion towards accomplishing objectives. Instead of survey deterrents as barriers, the section presents them as any open doors for development and learning. Perusers are outfitted with critical thinking methodologies and strategies for keeping up with inspiration notwithstanding misfortune, transforming hindrances into impetuses for strength and development.

Observing Achievements

The last point underscores the significance of perceiving and praising achievements along the way. Recognizing progress, regardless of how little, fills in as a strong inspiration and supports our obligation to our objectives. This part gives suggestions for commending accomplishments in manners that are significant and lined up with one's qualities, cultivating a feeling of achievement and empowerment, and proceeding with exertion towards a definitive vision.

In the long run, putting forth and accomplishing significant objectives is a powerful cycle that requires lucidity, arranging, perseverance, and flexibility. By embracing the standards illustrated in this part, perusers are engaged to focus on aggressive objectives, explore the difficulties that emerge with certainty, and, at last, understand their maximum capacity.

Developing self-control and consistency

The bedrock of supported inspiration and accomplishment lies not in that frame of mind of motivation but rather in the consistent, steady force of self-restraint and consistency. This part digs into the basic job these components play in changing dreams into the real world, directing perusers through the development of propensities that encourage a restrained way to deal with life and work.

The Embodiment of Self-Control

Self-control is understood as the capacity to seek after one's thought process, regardless of impulses to forsake it. Pursuing decisions line up with our objectives and values, in any event, when they struggle with quick longings or motivations. This segment investigates the mental underpinnings of self-control, including resolution, and the manners by which it tends to be reinforced over the long haul, similar to a muscle. Through down-to-earth guidance and activities, perusers are urged to recognize regions in their lives where self-restraint could prompt better progress and satisfaction.

Building Consistency Through Everyday Practice

Consistency is the regular ally of self-control; it transforms activities into propensities and objectives into accomplishments. This piece underscores the significance of laying out schedules that line up with one's objectives, subsequently making consistency a result of day-to-day existence. It examines how the impact of trained instinct can assist with bypassing the requirement for consistent determination as activities become programmed reactions to prompts in our current circumstances. Methodologies for making and adhering to schedules that help one's objectives are given, offering a plan for implanting consistency into the texture of day-to-day existence.

The Job of Responsibility

Responsibility is introduced as a basic part of keeping up with self-restraint and consistency. Whether through self-observing, objective setting, or enrolling the help of companions, family, or coaches, making an arrangement of responsibility guarantees that one remaining part is on target towards accomplishing their goals. This segment frames different strategies for laying out responsibility, including the utilization of innovation, social help, and individual reflection, to keep inspiration high and progress consistent.

Conquering Dawdling and Interruptions

A typical boundary between self-restraint and consistency is the propensity to linger or surrender to interruptions. This section tends to tackle these difficulties head-on, offering bits of knowledge into why we delay and how interruptions can crash our best aims. Pragmatic tips and techniques are given to beat these deterrents, like breaking errands into more modest, more reasonable pieces, setting clear cutoff times, and establishing a climate helpful for concentration and efficiency.

Observing Discipline and Consistency

At long last, the significance of perceiving and praising the job of self-restraint and consistency in making progress is highlighted. This part urges perusers to consider how far they have gotten through their restrained endeavors and reliable activities, recommending ways of commending these triumphs, both of all shapes and sizes. By recognizing the difficult work and commitment it takes to seek after one's objectives, perusers are helped to remember their solidarity and versatility, energizing their inspiration to progress forward with their way.

Taking everything into account, this section highlights the groundbreaking effect of self-control and consistency on making enduring progress and satisfaction. By embracing these standards and incorporating them into their day-to-day existence, perusers are furnished with the apparatuses expected to explore the excursion towards their objectives earnestly and with elegance.

Embracing Disappointment as a Venturing Stone to Progress

Chasing objectives and dreams, disappointment is an inescapable buddy. However, not the presence of disappointment characterizes our excursion, but our reaction to it. This part reevaluates disappointment as a chance, yet a fundamental venturing stone to progress. It guides perusers through the most common way of embracing disappointment, gaining from it, and involving it as an impetus for development and versatility.

The Truth of Disappointment

The part starts by standing up to the feeling of dread toward disappointment head-on, recognizing it as a widespread encounter. It dispels the legend that achievement is a direct path without difficulties. Through convincing accounts and examination, this segment represents how disappointment is a fundamental piece of the educational experience, giving significant bits of knowledge and illustrations that prepare for future accomplishments. By tolerating disappointment as a characteristic result of endeavor, we can reduce its ability to beat us down.

Gaining from Each Mishap

The core of this section lies in the methodologies for removing astuteness from disappointment. It presents an orderly way to deal with examining difficulties, empowering perusers to pose testing inquiries that uncover what turned out badly, why it worked out, and how comparative missteps can be kept away from now on. This part stresses the significance of keeping a development outlook, where moves are viewed as any open doors to extend one's capacities and information.

Flexibility: The Craft of Returning

Building flexibility is key to transforming disappointment into a springboard for progress. This part dives into the characteristics that make people tough, like good faith, flexibility, and determination. It offers reasonable guidance for developing these characteristics, including procedures for dealing with feelings, rethinking pessimistic contemplations, and keeping a drawn-out viewpoint. Through strength, we learn not exclusively to endure disappointments but to flourish in their result.

Incorporating disappointment into your example of overcoming adversity

This section urges perusers to incorporate their encounters with disappointment into their own stories of accomplishment. It investigates how recapping accounts of beating obstructions can move and rouse, both by and by and for other people. By purchasing and sharing our disappointments, we add to a culture that values learning and steadiness over flawlessness. This segment gives direction on the best way to convey these accounts in a way that features strength and development instead of rout.

Pushing Ahead with Certainty

In closing the part, the center moves to how we can push ahead with certainty in the wake of encountering disappointment. It highlights the significance of putting forth new objectives, equipped with the experiences and strength acquired from past mishaps. By reviewing disappointment as an impermanent condition as opposed to an extremely durable state, we can move toward future undertakings with restored force and assurance. This last segment leaves perusers with procedures for keeping up with energy, even notwithstanding misfortune, guaranteeing that disappointment turns into an incredible asset in their ammunition stockpile for making progress.

Generally, this section changes the idea of disappointment from a dreaded finish to an indispensable, improving piece of the excursion toward progress. By embracing disappointment, gaining from it, and building flexibility, perusers are prepared to explore the promising and less promising times of their interests with beauty and certainty, nearer and nearer to their most useful and satisfied selves.

Conclusion

Pondering the Excursion

As we wind down the extraordinary endeavor that is "The 5 AM Supernatural occurrence," it's important to stop and think about the excursion embraced. This snapshot of reflection isn't simply a regressive look; it is a festival of the steps made, the obstacles that survive, and the development of our most useful selves.

From the underlying test of ascending with the sunrise to incorporating the mainstays of wellbeing, health, and care into each feature of our day-to-day schedules, each step has been an intentional step towards understanding our undiscovered possibility. You've not just figured out how to welcome the morning with excitement yet have additionally become the best at focusing on, objectively setting, and utilizing innovation, all while cultivating versatility and flexibility.

This direct in the end is a greeting toward recognizing your development. Have you seen a change in your efficiency levels? Are mornings presently not a scramble against time, but rather a serene time of purposefulness? Maybe your objectives are more clear, your means towards them are more conscious, and your misfortunes are seen not as disappointments but rather as examples. This reflection is as much about commending the successes for all intents and purposes as it is about perceiving the regions where the excursion was testing, understanding that each stagger was a learning opportunity.

Pondering the excursion likewise implies valuing the significant impact on mentality that has happened. The faith in the chance of change and the comprehension that efficiency is certainly not a natural ability yet an expertise sharpened through discipline and commitment denote a critical shift. It's tied in with understanding that the supernatural occurrence of the 5 AM start isn't in the actual hour, but in what it addresses: a pledge to personal development, a demonstration of the force of schedule, and an image of the discipline it takes to accomplish our fantasies.

As you consider the way you've voyaged, recall that the excursion doesn't end here. The illustrations taken in, the propensities shaped, and the mentality shifts experienced are devices that will keep on serving you quite a ways past the extent of this book. The 5 AM supernatural occurrence isn't simply a routine; it's a way of life that persistently develops as you do.

At this time of reflection, invest heavily in how far you've come. The early mornings, the restrained schedules, and the objectives accomplished are demonstrations of your commitment. You've set out on this excursion to upgrade your efficiency as well as to open a form of yourself that flourishes while chasing greatness. This reflection isn't an end yet, but an achievement in the continuous excursion of development and self-revelation.

The Nonstop Idea of Progress

Leaving on the way framed in "The 5 AM Wonder" isn't an excursion with a conclusive endpoint, but a never-ending journey towards discipline and upgraded efficiency. This part fills in as an update that the mission for development is a continuous cycle, a consistent pattern of getting the hang of, adjusting, and developing.

Deep-rooted learning

The rule of long-lasting learning remains at the center of consistent improvement. Our general surroundings are in a steady state of motion, with new data, innovations, and systems arising at a quick speed. Remaining focused on learning guarantees that we stay versatile and creative, fit for exploring the intricacies of current life, and work with nimbleness and prescience. This segment urges perusers to develop an inquisitive mentality, one that searches out new information and encounters as wellsprings of motivation and development.

The Flexibility Variable

Improvement additionally relies on our capacity to adjust —tto turn in light of life's unavoidable changes and difficulties. This flexibility isn't tied to failing to focus on our objectives, but rather to being adaptable in our techniques to accomplish them. Whether it's changing our schedules to oblige another profession, embracing new advancements to improve our efficiency, or reexamining our objectives to line up with developing needs, versatility guarantees that we stay on the way to progress, no matter what the snags that emerge.

Refinement and enhancement

The excursion towards our most useful selves is likewise set apart by nonstop refinement and streamlining. As we develop and advance, so do our necessities and goals.

This piece of the section underlines the significance of consistently evaluating and refining our schedules, propensities, and objectives to guarantee they serve our ongoing selves. It's about adjusting our systems to expand productivity and viability, guaranteeing that our endeavors yield the best conceivable return.

Embracing Change

Integral to the idea of consistent improvement is the idea of progress. Change, however frequently overwhelming, is the main steady in the excursion of development. The impetus impels us out of our usual range of familiarity and into new domains of plausibility. This segment investigates how embracing change—nnot as a power to be opposed but rather as a valuable chance to be seized—ccan prompt significant individual and expert turns of events.

The way ahead

As we finish up this section, we are reminded that the way ahead isn't direct yet a twisting, driving us to ever-more prominent levels of information, capacity, and satisfaction. The consistent idea of progress intends that there is dependably one more level to take a stab at, one more limit to push. It welcomes us to see every day not as a redundancy of the last but rather as a new chance to learn, adjust, refine, and embrace the change that drives us forward.

Basically, the excursion of progress is endless, an interminable mission towards turning into the best version of ourselves. It is an excursion checked not by an objective but rather by the achievements we accomplish and the examples we advance en route. As we keep on exploring this way, let us do so with the comprehension that each step made is a stride towards a more useful, satisfied, and deliberate life.

The Job of the Local Area and Backing

In the odyssey towards understanding our fullest potential, the job of local area and backing arises as a signal of light, directing us through the unavoidable rhythmic movements of inspiration and discipline. This section highlights the priceless job that a steady local area plays in the excursion of change that "The 5 AM Supernatural occurrence" advocates.

The way to turning into our most useful selves is seldom strolled alone. En route, the consolation, intelligence, and responsibility presented by others can enlighten our means, making the excursion more tolerable as well as seriously advancing. This segment digs into the significance of encircling ourselves with similar people who share our obligation to development and improvement. Whether a tutor guides us, a companion who strolls next to us, or a local area that upholds us, the aggregate strength and shared encounters of others are strong impetuses for our own turn of events.

Drawing in with a local area of individual go-getters and efficiency searchers offers something beyond moral help; it gives a stage to trading thoughts, systems, and bits of knowledge that can upgrade our own schedules and approaches. This part urges perusers to effectively search out or make such networks, whether through web-based discussions, nearby gatherings, or informal communities committed to self-improvement and efficiency.

Also, the job of responsibility couldn't possibly be more significant. Having somebody to impart our objectives to, who will monitor our advancement and hold us to our responsibilities, fundamentally improves the probability of accomplishing our targets. This segment offers down-to-earth guidance on laying out responsibility organizations and how to capitalize on these connections, guaranteeing they are commonly useful and zeroing in on encouraging feedback.

The excursion towards morning authority and the past is advanced by the narratives, difficulties, and triumphs of others. This part highlights the significance of sharing our own encounters, adding to the aggregate information and support of the local area. By offering our experiences and gaining from those of others, we establish a powerful climate where development is duplicated and mishaps are viewed as shared difficulties instead of individual disappointments.

In closing this investigation of local area and backing, obviously the excursion to opening our most useful selves is as much about interfacing with others as it's worth about private discipline and inspiration. The securities shaped, the exhortation traded, and the responsibility shared are the strings that weave the texture of a steady local area, making each step towards our objectives more educated, more motivated, and more feasible.

Embracing change and flexibility

In the developing story of our efficiency process, the ability to embrace change and flexibility arises as a basic subject. This section digs into the intrinsic dynamism of life and work, recognizing that the main thing we can really expect is change itself. It's in this motion that our capacity to stay adaptable, to turn when fundamental, and to constantly adjust our activities to our advancing objectives becomes principal.

The Idea of Progress

Life's penchant for startling, exciting bends in the road can deliver even the most carefully laid plans out of date. This part presents the idea of progress not as an impediment to be dreaded but rather as a chance to be seized. It highlights the significance of keeping an outlook that is open to change and prepared to embrace the movements that life perpetually presents. By using survey change as an impetus for development, we can change possible interruptions into strong motors for individual and expert turns of events.

The specialty of versatility

Flexibility is the normal partner to change. The quality empowers us to explore life's vulnerabilities with effortlessness and flexibility. This part investigates procedures for developing versatility, for example, remaining informed about patterns in our businesses, developing a different range of abilities, and figuring out how to expect and plan for numerous results. Through down-to-earth activities and reflections, perusers are urged to foster the adaptability expected to flourish in an always-evolving climate.

Lining up with Advancing Objectives

As our lives change, so do our objectives and desires. This fragment tends to emphasize the significance of consistently evaluating and realigning our targets with our ongoing reality. It examines the benefit of providing an opportunity for reflection, permitting us to survey what's working, what isn't, and what changes should be made to our systems and schedules. This course of persistent realignment guarantees that our endeavors are constantly coordinated towards the most pertinent and significant objectives.

Exploring Mishaps with Spryness

Even with change, mishaps are inescapable. This section underlines the significance of answering these difficulties with readiness, transforming expected barriers into diversions instead of impasses. By embracing a critical thinking outlook and survey mishaps as any open doors to learn and develop, we can keep up with force and keep advancing towards our objectives, in any event, when the way becomes hazy.

The Persistent Excursion of Development

The part finishes up by supporting the excursion towards augmenting efficiency, and it is progressing to understand our true capacity. Embracing change and versatility is definitely not a one-time task, but rather a consistent effort. It's tied in with staying open to new encounters, remaining adaptable despite vulnerability, and being willing to advance as our conditions and desires change.

Generally, embracing change and versatility is tied in with perceiving that the way to our most useful selves isn't direct yet liquid. It's an excursion set apart by development, learning, and the consistent recalibration of our objectives and techniques. By developing a mentality that invites change and values flexibility, we furnish ourselves with the instruments expected to explore the intricacies of life and work with certainty and reason.

Pushing Ahead with a Recharged Reason

As we approach the end of "The 5 AM Marvel: Opening Your Generally Useful Self," it's basic to project our look forward, equipped with the apparatuses, bits of knowledge, and encounters gathered from our excursion. This last section isn't only a nearby yet a takeoff platform into a future where the standards of discipline, development, and care illuminate each perspective regarding our lives.

The embodiment of pushing ahead lies in conveying the illustrations of the 5 AM supernatural occurrence into every day with reestablished reason. You've stirred to the force of early mornings, embraced the discipline expected for significant self-awareness, and seen the extraordinary impacts of steady exertion and positive mentality. Presently, the way forward is yours to shape, with every early daytime offering a new material whereupon to make your show-stopper of efficiency and satisfaction.

Embracing the excursion ahead requires a pledge to non-stop improvement. The standards spread out in this book are not static; they are intended to advance as you do. As you experience new difficulties, yearnings, and amazing open doors, the adaptability to adjust your schedules, objectives, and procedures will be central. The 5 AM supernatural occurrence is a system for living, one that upholds your development and develops with your excursion.

In addition, the excursion forward is enhanced by the soul of investigation. The interest in attempting new practices, the mental fortitude to step outside your usual range of familiarity, and the readiness to embrace change are the signs of a day-to-day existence lived completely. Whether it's exploring different avenues regarding different morning schedules, investigating new regions for self-improvement, or laying out progressively aggressive objectives, the quest for development is perpetual and elating.

As you push ahead, make sure to stop and reflect consistently. Reflection is the compass that directs your excursion, assisting you to remain lined up with your qualities, gain from your encounters, and value your advancement. Through reflection, you'll track down clarity, inspiration, and the solidarity to continue through difficulties.

Finally, pushing ahead with recharged reason implies living with deliberateness. settling on cognizant decisions that mirror your needs, values, and objectives. Each activity, each choice, and each day is a chance to live intentionally, to impact your life into an impression of your most elevated desires.

All things considered, the excursion of "The 5 AM Wonder" is just the start. Ahead lies a long period of mornings, each offering the commitment of progress, development, and revelation. Equipped with the standards of discipline, care, and intentional living, you are ready to open up to your most useful self, yet your most satisfied and significant life. Here's to pushing ahead, to the supernatural occurrences that anticipate with each new day break.